CW00346586

by Iain Gray

Lang**Syne**
PUBLISHING
WRITING *to* REMEMBER

WRITING *to* REMEMBER

79 Main Street, Newtongrange,
Midlothian EH22 4NA
Tel: 0131 344 0414   Fax: 0845 075 6085
E-mail: info@lang-syne.co.uk
www.langsyneshop.co.uk

Design by Dorothy Meikle
Printed by Printwell Ltd
© Lang Syne Publishers Ltd 2019

ISBN 978-1-85217-517-7

Holmes

MOTTO:
Trust, but in whom take care.

CREST:
The head of a lion.

NAME variations include:
Holme
Holms
Hulme
Hulmes

Chapter one:

The origins of popular surnames

by George Forbes and Iain Gray

If you don't know where you came from, you won't know where you're going is a frequently quoted observation and one that has a particular resonance today when there has been a marked upsurge in interest in genealogy, with increasing numbers of people curious to trace their family roots.

Main sources for genealogical research include census returns and official records of births, marriages and deaths – and the key to unlocking the detail they contain is obviously a family surname, one that has been 'inherited' and passed from generation to generation.

No matter our station in life, we all have a surname – but it was not until about the middle of the fourteenth century that the practice of being identified by a particular surname became commonly established throughout the British Isles.

Previous to this, it was normal for a person to be identified through the use of only a forename.

But as population gradually increased and there were many more people with the same forename, surnames were adopted to distinguish one person, or community, from another.

Many common English surnames are patronymic in origin, meaning they stem from the forename of one's father – with 'Johnson,' for example, indicating 'son of John.'

It was the Normans, in the wake of their eleventh century conquest of Anglo-Saxon England, a pivotal moment in the nation's history, who first brought surnames into usage – although it was a gradual process.

For the Normans, these were names initially based on the title of their estates, local villages and chateaux in France to distinguish and identify these landholdings.

Such grand descriptions also helped enhance the prestige of these warlords and generally glorify their lofty positions high above the humble serfs slaving away below in the pecking order who had only single names, often with Biblical connotations as in Pierre and Jacques.

The only descriptive distinctions among the peasantry concerned their occupations, like 'Pierre the swineherd' or 'Jacques the ferryman.'

Roots of surnames that came into usage in England not only included Norman-French, but also Old French, Old Norse, Old English, Middle English, German, Latin, Greek, Hebrew and the Gaelic languages of the Celts.

The Normans themselves were originally Vikings, or 'Northmen', who raided, colonised and eventually settled down around the French coastline.

The had sailed up the Seine in their longboats in 900AD under their ferocious leader Rollo and ruled the roost in north eastern France before sailing over to conquer England in 1066 under Duke William of Normandy – better known to posterity as William the Conqueror, or King William I of England.

Granted lands in the newly-conquered England, some of their descendants later acquired territories in Wales, Scotland and Ireland – taking not only their own surnames, but also the practice of adopting a surname, with them.

But it was in England where Norman rule and custom first impacted, particularly in relation to the adoption of surnames.

This is reflected in the famous *Domesday Book*, a massive survey of much of England and Wales, ordered by William I, to determine who owned what, what it was worth and therefore how much they were liable to pay in taxes to the voracious Royal Exchequer.

Completed in 1086 and now held in the National Archives in Kew, London, 'Domesday' was an Old English word meaning 'Day of Judgement.'

This was because, in the words of one contemporary chronicler, "its decisions, like those of the Last Judgement, are unalterable."

It had been a requirement of all those English landholders – from the richest to the poorest – that they identify themselves for the purposes of the survey and for future reference by means of a surname.

This is why the *Domesday Book*, although written in Latin as was the practice for several centuries with both civic and ecclesiastical records, is an invaluable source for the early appearance of a wide range of English surnames.

Several of these names were coined in connection with occupations.

These include Baker and Smith, while Cooks, Chamberlains, Constables and Porters were to be found carrying out duties in large medieval households.

The church's influence can be found in names such as Bishop, Friar and Monk while the popular name of Bennett derives from the late fifth to mid-sixth century Saint Benedict, founder of the Benedictine order of monks.

The early medical profession is represented by Barber, while businessmen produced names that include Merchant and Sellers.

Down at the village watermill, the names that cropped up included Millar/Miller, Walker and Fuller, while other self-explanatory trades included Cooper, Tailor, Mason and Wright.

Even the scenery was utilised as in Moor, Hill, Wood and Forrest – while the hunt and the chase supplied names that include Hunter, Falconer, Fowler and Fox.

Colours are also a source of popular surnames, as in Black, Brown, Gray/Grey, Green and White, and would have denoted the colour of the clothing the person habitually wore or, apart from the obvious exception of 'Green', one's hair colouring or even complexion.

The surname Red developed into Reid, while

Blue was rare and no-one wanted to be associated with yellow.

Rather self-important individuals took surnames that include Goodman and Wiseman, while physical attributes crept into surnames such as Small and Little.

Many families proudly boast the heraldic device known as a Coat of Arms, as featured on our front cover.

The central motif of the Coat of Arms would originally have been what was borne on the shield of a warrior to distinguish himself from others on the battlefield.

Not featured on the Coat of Arms, but high-lighted on page three, is the family motto and related crest – with the latter frequently different from the central motif.

Adding further variety to the rich cultural heritage that is represented by surnames is the appearance in recent times in lists of the 100 most common names found in England of ones that include Khan, Patel and Singh – names that have proud roots in the vast sub-continent of India.

Echoes of a far distant past can still be found in our surnames and they can be borne with pride in commemoration of our forebears.

Chapter two:

On the high seas

A name with a number of possible sources of origin, 'Holmes' is of ancient Anglo-Saxon roots and derives from both 'holm', indicating someone who lived near a holly tree, and the Old English 'holen', denoting someone who lived on, or near, a slightly raised islet.

With roots that also include the Old Norse 'holmr', its Anglicised-Gaelic forms are Mac Thomáis and Mac Thámáis, sometimes rendered as Cavish.

With variations of the popular name that include Holme and Hulme, it first appeared in the present-day English county of Lancashire and is firmly identified with Anglo-Saxon culture.

Flowing through the veins of many people of English birth today such as bearers of the Holmes name is the blood of those Germanic tribes who invaded and settled in the south and east of the island of Britain from about the early fifth century.

Known as the Anglo-Saxons, they were composed of the Jutes, from the area of the Jutland Peninsula in modern Denmark, the Saxons from

Lower Saxony, in modern Germany and the Angles from the Angeln area of Germany.

It was the Angles who gave the name 'Engla land', or 'Aengla land' – better known as 'England.'

They held sway in what became England from approximately 550 to 1066, with the main kingdoms those of Sussex, Wessex, Northumbria, Mercia, Kent, East Anglia and Essex.

Whoever controlled the most powerful of these kingdoms was tacitly recognised as overall 'king' – one of the most noted being Alfred the Great, King of Wessex from 871 to 899.

It was during his reign that the famous *Anglo-Saxon Chronicle* was compiled – an invaluable source of Anglo-Saxon history – while Alfred was designated in early documents as *Rex Anglorum Saxonum*, King of the English Saxons.

Through the Anglo-Saxons, the language known as Old English developed, later transforming from the eleventh century into Middle English – sources from which many popular English surnames of today, such as Holmes, derive.

The Anglo-Saxons meanwhile, had usurped the power of the indigenous Britons – who referred to them as 'Saeson' or 'Saxones.'

It is from this that the Scottish Gaelic term for 'English people' of 'Sasannach' derives, the Irish Gaelic 'Sasanach' and the Welsh 'Saeson.'

We learn from the *Anglo-Saxon Chronicle* how the religion of the early Anglo-Saxons was one that pre-dated the establishment of Christianity in the British Isles.

Known as a form of Germanic paganism, with roots in Old Norse religion, it shared much in common with the Druidic 'nature-worshipping' religion of the indigenous Britons.

It was in the closing years of the sixth century that Christianity began to take a hold in Britain, while by approximately 690 it had become the 'established' religion of Anglo-Saxon England.

Following the battle of Hastings in October of 1066, that saw the death of Harold II, last of the Anglo-Saxon kings, William Duke of Normandy was declared King of England on December 25, and the complete subjugation of his Anglo-Saxon subjects followed.

Those Normans who had fought on his behalf were rewarded with the lands of Anglo-Saxons, many of whom sought exile abroad as mercenaries.

Within an astonishingly short space of time, Norman manners, customs and law were imposed on England – laying the basis for what subsequently became established 'English' custom and practice.

But beneath the surface, old Anglo-Saxon culture was not totally eradicated.

Some aspects were absorbed into those of the Normans, while faint echoes of the Anglo-Saxon past is still seen today in the form of popular surnames such as Holmes.

Bearers of this proud name figure prominently in the historical record.

One particularly flamboyant and adventurous character was Sir Robert Holmes, the English Admiral who not only participated in two wars against the Dutch but was also responsible for sparking off the wars in the first place.

Born in 1622, the son of a wealthy English landowner who owned an estate at Mallow, in the Irish county of Cork, he was a staunch Royalist during the English Civil War.

The monarch Charles I had incurred the wrath of Parliament by his insistence on the 'divine right' of monarchs, and added to this was Parliament's fear of Catholic 'subversion' against the state and the king's stubborn refusal to grant demands for religious and constitutional concessions.

Matters came to a head with the outbreak of the Civil War in 1642, with Parliamentary forces, known as the New Model Army and commanded by Oliver Cromwell and Sir Thomas Fairfax, arrayed against the Royalist army of the king.

In what became an increasingly bloody and complex conflict, spreading to Scotland and Ireland and with rapidly shifting loyalties on both sides, the king was eventually captured and executed in January of 1649 on the orders of Parliament.

Holmes had served as a Cornet in the Prince Maurice Regiment of Horse and, a year before the king's execution, came into contact with the section of the English naval fleet that had defected to the Royalist cause.

Taking to the high seas with the Royalist fleet, he took part in its epic cruise from 1649 to the Mediterranean, West Africa and the West Indies.

Acting immediately before the Restoration of Charles II in 1660 as a courier between the exiled king and his supporters in England, he was later rewarded with the command of a naval expedition to the Guinea Coast, then in Dutch hands.

Capturing a number of Dutch vessels and also Dutch territory, this is why Holmes is considered to have been responsible for the Second Anglo-Dutch War of 1665 to 1667.

In 1666, in what is known as *Holmes's Bonfire*, he launched an attack on Dutch merchant ships, destroying 150 of them and sacking the Dutch town of West Terschelling.

Similar actions against Dutch mercantile interests on the part of the daring and freebooting Holmes, who by this time had been promoted to the rank of Admiral by a grateful English nation, also sparked off the Third Anglo-Dutch War of 1672 to 1674.

He died in 1692, while he was also the grandfather of the equally distinguished Rear Admiral Charles Holmes, born in 1711 and who played a leading role during the Seven Years War of 1756 to 1763 against French interests in North America.

Third in command to General James Wolfe during the capture of Quebec from the French in 1759, a year earlier he led a squadron up the River Ems, leading to the capture of the fortified garrison of Emden.

Later appointed Commander-in-Chief at Jamaica, he died there in 1761, while there is a memorial to him in Westminster Abbey, London.

Chapter three:

Honours and distinction

In later centuries, and on much different fields of battle, bearers of the Holmes name have also gained distinction – with no fewer than four being recipients of the Victoria Cross (VC), the highest award for valour in the face of enemy action for British and Commonwealth forces.

Born in 1821 in Halifax, Yorkshire, Joel Holmes was a recipient of the honour during the Indian Mutiny of 1857 to 1858.

He had been a private in the 84th Regiment, York and Lancaster Regiment, when, in September of 1857 at Lucknow, he volunteered under heavy fire to operate a gun from which nearly all the artillerymen had already been killed or wounded.

He died in 1872, while his VC is now on display at the York and Lancaster Regiment Museum in Rotherham, South Yorkshire.

In the terrible carnage that was the First World War of 1914 to 1918, Frederick Holmes, born in 1889 in Bermondsey, London, was also a recipient of the VC.

He had been a lance corporal in the 2nd Battalion, The King's Own Yorkshire Light Infantry when, in August of 1914 at Le Cateau, France, he braved heavy enemy fire to rescue a wounded comrade from the trenches and later helped to drive a gun out of action by taking the place of its wounded driver.

Later promoted to the rank of captain, he died in 1969.

Born in 1895 in Wood Stanway, Gloucestershire, William Holmes was a posthumous recipient of the VC.

He had been a private in the 2nd Battalion, Grenadier Guards when, in October of 1918 at Cattenièrs, France, he was killed after rescuing a number of his wounded comrades under intense fire.

His VC is now on display at The Guards Regimental Headquarters (Grenadier Guards RHQ), Wellington Barracks, London.

Also on the battlefields of the First World War, Thomas Holmes is the youngest Canadian to have won the VC.

Born in Montreal, he had been a 19-year-old private in the 4th Canadian Mountain Rifles, 2nd Battalion, Canadian Expeditionary Force when, in October of 1917 near Passchendaele, Belgium, he single-handedly eliminated the crews of two enemy machine-gun nests.

He died in 1950 – fifteen years, sadly, after his VC was stolen in a robbery at his home.

Taking to the skies above London during the Second World War, Raymond Tower Holmes, better known as Ray Holmes, born in Liverpool in 1914, was the British fighter pilot hailed by the press at the time as a war hero after saving Buckingham Palace from severe damage during a German bombing raid over central London.

It had been as an RAF sergeant flying a Hawker Hurricane fighter that, in September of 1940 during the Battle of Britain, he spotted a Dornier Do17 bomber attempting a bombing run over the palace.

Attacking the German heavy bomber head-on, his machine-guns suddenly failed. Undaunted, however, he rammed the aircraft – cutting off its tail and causing it to crash near Victoria tube station.

With his own aircraft severely damaged, he managed to successfully bail out before it plummeted to earth near the grounds of Buckingham Palace.

Sixty-five years later, in 2005, the wreckage of his fighter was located and excavated from the streets of London and formed the subject of the fascinating National Geographic Channel documentary *The Search for the Lost Fighter Plane*.

Serving later as a trusted King's Messenger, personally delivering mail to Prime Minister Winston Churchill, he died in the same year that the documentary was released.

Born in 1946 in Aldridge, Staffordshire, Richard Holmes was the former soldier and distinguished military historian who, before his death in 2011, had become noted for a series of popular British television war documentaries that include *War Walks* and *Battlefields*.

A former brigadier in the Territorial Army, he served as a co-director of Cranfield University's Security Studies Institute at the Royal College of Military Science, Shrivenham.

He was also editor-in-chief of the Oxford University Press *Companion to Military History*.
One British soldier with a particularly unusual claim to fame was Sergeant Alfred Holmes, born in the British possession of Gibraltar, near Spain, in 1931.

Enlisting in the Gibraltar Regiment in the 1950s he was appointed to the official post of Officer-in Charge of the Apes – as the Macaques monkeys were then known.

This is a post that dated back to 1913, ending three years before Holmes' death in 1994, when the care of the Gibraltar Barbary Macaques monkeys was the responsibility of the British Army.

Over a period of more than 38 years, Sergeant Holmes fed and nursed them and generally cared for their well-being.

He became so well-known and respected by the native Gibraltarians that he was known in Spanish as *El de los monos – He of the monkeys*.

Bearers of the Holmes name have also gained distinction in the world of medicine.

Born in 1797 in Cadiz, Spain, to Thomas Holmes and Susanna Scott but later settling in Montreal, Andrew Holmes was the Canadian physician and academic who, in 1823, co-founded the Montreal Medical Institution, Canada's first medical school.

This was after studying and qualifying as a medical doctor from the University of Edinburgh, Scotland.

Returning to Canada, he joined the staff of the Montreal General Hospital in 1822.

The Montreal Medical Institution that he co-founded with John Stephenson later joined with

McGill College to become the centre of medical excellence known today as Montreal's McGill College Medical Faculty, part of McGill University.

He died in 1860, while it is in his honour that the Holmes Gold Medal is awarded annually by the university to the medical student who achieves the highest academic standing upon graduation.

Born in 1890 in Low Fell, Gateshead, Arthur Holmes was the pioneering British geologist who, in his famous 1913 booklet *The Age of the Earth*, estimated the planet's age based on highly complex studies of the abundance of uranium isotopes.

Holding the chair of geology at the University of Edinburgh from 1943, he was also the author of the 1944 *Principles of Physical Geography*; he died in 1965.

The Arthur Holmes Medal of the European Geosciences Union is named for him as is also a crater on Mars.

Across the Atlantic from the original Holmes homeland of England, Oliver Wendell Holmes and his son Oliver Wendell Holmes, Jr., figure prominently in the historical record of the United States.

Born in 1809 in Cambridge, Massachusetts, Holmes senior was not only a pioneering medical doctor but is also regarded as one of America's leading literary figures.

Qualifying as a doctor from Harvard Medical School in 1836, he later became an expert on the causes of, and treatment for, puerperal fever.

In addition to his medical accomplishments, he became a member of what is known as America's highly popular *Fireside Poets* – producing many works of both verse and prose that include his *'Breakfast-Table'* series – most notably his 1858 *The Autocrat of the Breakfast-Table*.

He died in 1894, while his son, Oliver Wendell Homes, Jr., born in 1841, was the leading American jurist who, from 1902 to 1932, served as an Associate Justice of the Supreme Court of the United States.

Responsible for coining the term "clear and present danger" with reference to any acts that threatened the United States and its citizens, he died in 1935 – while he was also portrayed by the actor Louis Calhern in two separate films of the same name –the 1946 and the 1950 *The Magnificent Yankee*.

Chapter four:

On the world stage

First gaining fame for her role from 1998 to 2003 of Joey Potter in the television teen drama Dawson's Creek, Katie Holmes is the American actress born in 1978 in Toledo, Ohio.

Married from 2006 to 2012 to the actor Tom Cruise, her big screen credits include the 2002 *Abandon* and the 2005 *Batman Begins*, while in 2011 she played the role of Jackie Kennedy in the bio-pic *The Kennedys*.

Born in 1950 in Encino, California, **Dennis Holmes** is the former child actor who, from 1961 to 1963, played the role of the orphaned Mike Williams in the popular Western television series *Laramie*.

Best known for his role of Jack Stall in the 2005 film *A History of Violence*, **Ashton Holmes** is the television and film actor born in 1978 in Albany, New York.

Other screen credits include the television drama series *Revenge*, *Boston Legal*, *Nikita* and *Crime Scene Investigation*, while he also appeared in the 2010 Second World War series *Pacific*.

Born in 1967 in Rochdale, Lancashire, Corinne Michelle Cuncliffe is the English actress better known as **Michelle Holmes**.

Film credits include the role of Sue in the 1986 *Rita, Sue and Bob Too*, while television credits include *Coronation Street*, *Emmerdale*, *Shameless* and *Goodnight Sweetheart*.

Born in Belfast in 1959, **Eamonn Holmes** is the journalist and radio and television personality who has hosted a host of popular television programmes that include *This Morning*.

In addition to having presented coverage of sports ranging from snooker and darts to horse racing, he has also, since 2005, been a presenter for Sky News.

Behind the camera lens, **Ben Holmes**, born in 1890 in Richmond, Virginia, and who died in 1943, was the American screenwriter and film director whose credits include the 1938 *The Saint in New York* and, from 1940, *The Saint's Double Trouble*.

Born in 1975 in Stratford upon Avon, **Jon Holmes** is the award-winning British comedian, writer and broadcaster who is one of the creators of the radio and television show *Dead Ringers*.

Other television writing credits include

Mock the Week, *Have I Got News for You* and *The Harry Hill Show*.

Bearers of the Holmes name have also excelled in the highly competitive world of sport.

Invested as a Dame Commander of the British Empire (DBE) in 2005, **Kelly Holmes** is the British retired middle-distance runner born in 1970 in Hildenborough, Kent.

Winner of a gold medal in both the 800-metres and 1500-metres events at the 2004 Olympics in Athens, she was a British Army physical training instructor before becoming a full-time athlete in 1997.

An inductee of the England Athletics Hall of Fame and voted BBC Sports Personality of the Year in 2004, she is also the founder of the registered charity the Dame Kelly Holmes Legacy (DKH Legacy), that supports young athletes.

On the water, **Andy Holmes** was the British rower born in 1959 in Uxbridge, London.

The recipient of an MBE, he was aged 19 when he won the Thames Challenge Cup at Henley Royal Regatta.

At Olympic level, he was a gold medallist in the Men's Coxless Fours in 1984 and also in the Men's Coxless Pairs in 1988.

He died in 2010, after contracting the water-borne disease Leptospirosis, more commonly known as Weil's disease.

Becoming blind when he was a promising young teenage swimmer, **Chris Holmes** nevertheless went on to win nine gold medals, five silver and one bronze representing Britain at all four Paralympic Games from 1988 to 2000.

Born in 1971, and the recipient of an MBE, the former swimmer has been a commissioner for the Disability Rights Commission while he was also Director of Paralympic Integration for the 2012 Olympics and Paralympics in London.

In the rough and tumble that is the game of rugby union, **Greg Holmes** is the Australian rugby prop capped thirteen times playing for his nation between 2005 and 2010.

Born in 1983 in Warwick, Queensland he has played for teams that include Sunnybank, Ballymore Tornadoes and, in international Super Rugby, the Queensland Reds.

Born to British parents in 1928 in Buenos Aires, Argentina, **William Holmes** was the rugby union player who played for both the England national team and the Argentina team.

Educated in Britain, he played for Cambridge University and was a full-back for England in the 1949 Five Nations Championship.

He returned to Argentina in the same year and was capped twice for them – but he died from typhoid fever only a few weeks later and less than a week after his marriage.

In the Canadian national sport of ice hockey, **Charles Holmes**, born in 1934 in Edmonton, Alberta, is the retired player who, in the 1950s and 1960s, played 23 games in the National Hockey League (NHL) for the Detroit Red Wings.

Born in 1899 in Portage la Prairie, Manitoba, **Bill Holmes** was the renowned ice hockey player who, between 1924 and 1936, played in the NHL for teams that include the Montreal Canadiens and New York Americans; he died in 1961.

Winner of ice hockey's prestigious Stanley Cup while playing between 1912 and 1928 for teams that include the Toronto Blueshirts, Toronto Arenas and Detroit Cougars, Harry Holmes, better known as **Hap Holmes**, was the player born in 1892 in Aurora, Ontario.

An inductee of the Hockey Hall of Fame, he died in 1941.

From sport to music, **Joe Holmes**, born in 1963 in New Jersey, is the American heavy metal guitarist who has played for bands and artistes who include Lizzy Borden, Dave Lee Roth and Ozzy Osbourne.

Taking to the heavens, **Edwin Holmes**, born in 1838, was the English amateur astronomer who in 1892 discovered the period comet that was named *17P/Holmes* in his honour.

A recipient of the Donohoe Comet Medal of the Astronomical Society of the Pacific, he died in 1919.

Responsible for coining the term 'travelogue', **Burton Holmes** was the American traveller, photographer and filmmaker born in Chicago in 1870.

Beginning his career as a travel lecturer, he later combined commentary along with film of his travels, producing what were the first travelogues.

Travelling extensively throughout North and South America, Europe, Russia and India he also shot the first films ever made of Japan, while he also shot popular travel films for both Paramount and MGM.

The recipient of a star on the Hollywood Walk of Fame, he died in 1958.

Born in 1923 in Louisville, Kentucky,

Martha Holmes, also known after her marriage to the theatrical executive Arthur Waxman as Martha Holmes Waxman, was an American photographer and journalist.

Working as a photographers' assistant on the *Louisville Courier-Journal* and *Louisville Times* and later as a photographer, she joined *Life* magazine in 1944 as one of its staff photographers in Washington, D.C.

Ranked as one of the top female photographers in America and with her photographs exhibited worldwide, her many famous subjects include the artist Jackson Pollock and Humphrey Bogart and Lauren Bacall.

Before her death in 2006 she memorably stated: "One thing *Life* always taught us: They'd say 'Film is cheap. Use it. Shoot, shoot, shoot.'"

In the field of medicine, **Hamilton E. Holmes** was the American orthopaedic surgeon born in 1941 in Atlanta, Georgia.

He and Charlayne Hunter-Gault were the first African-American students admitted to the University of Georgia, while he was the first African-American student to attend the Emory University School of Medicine.

Qualifying as a doctor in 1967, he later became a professor of orthopaedics and associate dean at Emory.

He died in 1995, while the first endowed professorship at the University of Georgia named for an African-American was created in his name in 1999.

With the plant *Euphorbia susanholmesiae* named in her honour, **Susan Carter Holmes** is the distinguished British botanist and taxonomist born in 1933.

Based at the Royal Botanic Gardens in Kew, London, and having discovered and catalogued more than 200 plants of the *Euphorbiaceous* family, she has served as president of the International Euphorbia Society.

An inductee of America's National Inventors Hall of Fame, **Dr Donald Holmes** was the organic chemist who in 1942, along with Dr William Hanford, invented the process for making the multi-purpose material polyurethane.

Born in 1910 in Woodbury, New Jersey, he died in 1980.

Another bearer of the Holmes name whose legacy survives to this day was the American businessman Edwin Holmes, who first commercialised the electromagnetic burglar alarm and established the first burglar alarm networks.

Born in 1820 in West Boylston, Massachusetts, he had been a seller of household goods when, in 1857, he bought the patent rights for a burglar alarm device that had been invented four years earlier by the Rev. Augustus Russell.

Moving to New York, and later explaining his move by describing the city as "where all the country's burglars made their home", by 1866 he had installed 1,200 home alarms in addition to marketing them among business enterprises.

In 1877, he established the first network of alarms in New York City monitored by a central station, while a year later he became president of the newly-established Bell Telephone Company; he died in 1901.

No historical narrative of proud bearers of the Holmes name could perhaps be complete without a reference to the most famous fictional character of the name.

This, of course, is **Sherlock Holmes**, the detective character created by Sir Arthur Conan Doyle and who first appeared in publication in 1887.